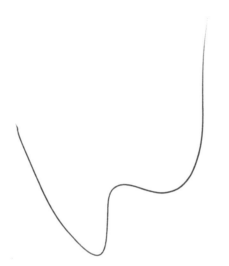

Pebble® Plus

Living or Non–living?

by Abbie Dunne

raintree
a Capstone company — publishers for children

Raintree is an imprint of Capstone Global Library Limited, a company incorporated in England and Wales having its registered office at 264 Banbury Road, Oxford, OX2 7DY – Registered company number: 6695582

www.raintree.co.uk
myorders@raintree.co.uk

Edited by Linda Staniford
Designed by Bobbie Nuytten
Picture research by Jo Miller
Production by Tori Abraham

ISBN 978-1-474-72251-3
20 19 18 17 16
10 9 8 7 6 5 4 3 2 1

British Library Cataloguing in Publication Data
A full catalogue record for this book is available from the British Library.

Acknowledgements
We would like to thank the following for permission to reproduce photographs: Shutterstock: Andresr, 5, ArTDi101, 9, BGSmith, 11, Bruce MacQueen, 13, Dave Allen Photography, 19, Dennis van de Water, 17, Eric Isselee, cover, Mny-Jhee, 1, Ozgur Coskun, 21, Richard A McMillian, 7, Shevs, 15

Design Elements
Shutterstock: Alena P

Printed and bound in China.

Contents

Living or non-living?

The world is full of life.

Take a deep breath! You are

a living human being.

Look around! Plants and

animals are living things too.

There are also many non-living things in the world. A ball and a bicycle are not alive. Rocks, sand, and water are non-living things too.

Energy

Living things need energy.

Plants make energy from sunlight,

air and water. They catch sunlight

on their leaves. Water and air enter

the plant through its leaves and roots.

Animals need energy too.
They eat food for their bodies
to make energy. Animals also
drink water and breathe air
to survive.

Moving and reacting

Living things move on
their own. Non-living things
cannot move on their own.
Plants shoot up from the soil.
Animals walk, run, fly or swim.

Living things react
to things around them.
Plants react by bending
toward sunlight. Animals
react with their senses.

Growing and reproducing

Living things reproduce. They
make more of their own kind.
Ducks lay eggs. Ducklings
grow up to be like their parents.
Non-living things cannot reproduce.

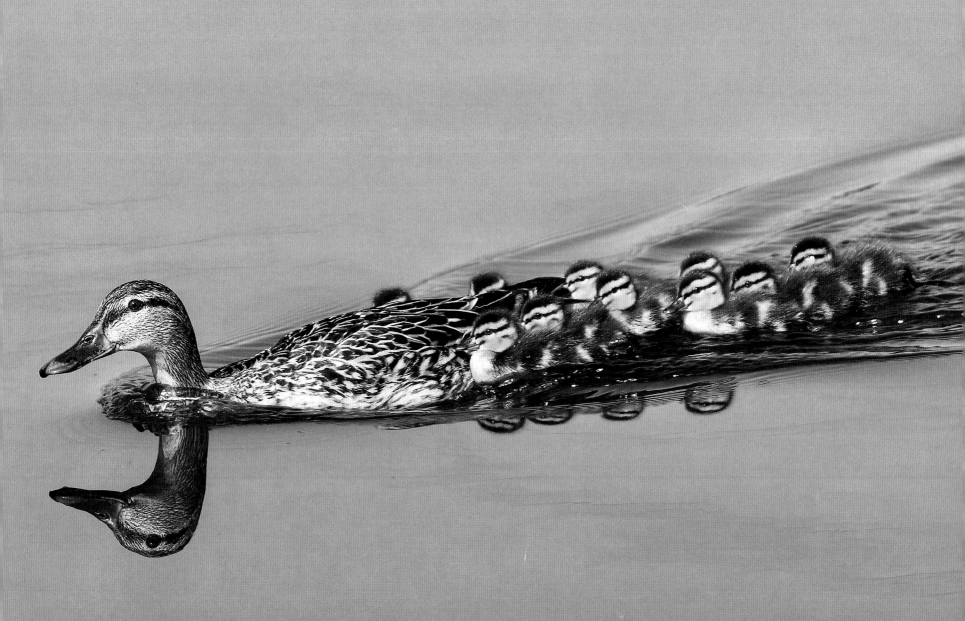

Living things grow and change.

Leaves grow and change colour.

Then they fall to the ground.

All living things grow old and die.

Activity

The world is full of living and non-living things. Find out how to tell the difference between them.

What you need

- pencil and paper
- area to survey

What you do

1. Make a table on a sheet of paper. It could look like this one. Add numbers to 20.

THING	ACTIONS	LIVING	NONLIVING
1.			
2.			
3.			
4.			
5.			

2. Pick 20 things you see around you.

3. In the Actions column, write down what each thing is doing on its own, or what you have seen it do on its own over time. If a thing does not do anything on its own, leave the Actions column blank.

4. Decide if the thing is living or non-living. Put a tick in that column.

What do you think?

Make a claim.

What is one way to tell the difference between living and nonliving things?

Use the results of your experiment to find out.

Glossary

energy the strength to do active things

living alive

non-living not alive; not having the qualities of living things

react act in response to something that happens

reproduce make offspring

root part of a plant that is underground

senses seeing, hearing, tasting, smelling and touching; using our senses helps us learn about our surroundings

survive stay alive

Find out more

Books

Living and Non-living in the Polar Regions (Is it Living or Non-living?), Rebecca Rissman (Raintree, 2013)

Living Things (Mind Webs), Anna Claybourne (Wayland, 2014)

What are Living and Nonliving Things? (Let's Find Out: Life Science), Louise Spilsbury (Britannica Educational Publishing in association with Rosen Educational Services, 2014)

Websites

www.bbc.co.uk/bitesize/ks1/science/living_things/play/

This site has games about living things.

http://www.educationquizzes.com/ks1/science/living-things-alive-or-not/

This is a quiz about whether things are alive or not.

www.bbc.co.uk/education/clips/zg7s39q

This video shows the difference between living and non-living things.

Comprehension questions

1. Name four things that a living thing needs to stay alive.

2. Living things react to changes around them. What do you think this means?

3. Is a tree living or non-living? How do you know?

4. Do you think a toy car is a living or non-living thing?

Index